CW00455234

Violin
Grade 6

Pieces
for Trinity College London exams

2016-2019

Published by
Trinity College London
www.trinitycollege.com

Registered in England
Company no. 02683033
Charity no. 1014792

Printed in England by Caligraving Ltd.

Preludio: Allegro

1st movement from Suite, op. 3 no. 4

Richard Jones
(died 1744)

2

Grazioso

2nd movement from Sonata in A, op. 4 no. 5

Simon Leduc
(1742-1777)

Grazioso [♩ = 76]

Second time:

to p. 16

D. C. al Fine

Danse Paysanne

Alfred Moffat
(1863-1950)

Only play the repeat at bars 55-62, and the D. S. al Fine.

6

D. S. al Fine

Allegro

1st movt from Sonata in E minor KV304

Wolfgang Amadeus Mozart
(1756-1791)

14

Intermezzo

from *Cavalleria Rusticana*

Pietro Mascagni
(1863-1945)

to p. 25

Pastoral

from *Four English Sketches*

William Hurlstone
(1876-1906)

Invitation to the Dance

Arr. by Polly Waterfield
and Timothy Kraemer

Hungarian traditional

Hora-Hatikvah

from *Israeli Concerto*

George Perlman
(1897-2000)

rit.

(Hatikvah)

28

Waltz

from *Sonata*

Virgil Thomson
(1896-1989)

* Lower notes may be omitted in these bars

(continued from inside front cover)

Technical work – Candidates to prepare i) Bowing exercise

i) Bowing exercise (from memory):

Candidates should play one of the Grade 6 scales, freely chosen from the list, with each note of the scale played as two spiccato quavers.
[♩ = 150]

Candidates to prepare in full *either* section ii) *or* section iii)

either **ii) Scales, arpeggios & technical exercises** (from memory):

Candidates should prepare major and minor scales and arpeggios from the following tonal centres, to be played with separate bows *or* slurred as requested by the examiner.

A	three octaves	min. tempi: scales: ♩ = 96 arpeggios: ♩. = 63 7ths: ♩ = 96	scales separate bows *or* slurred four crotchet beats to a bow; arpeggios separate bows *or* slurred three notes to a bow
F and Eb	two octaves		scales separate bows *or* slurred four crotchet beats to a bow; arpeggios separate bows *or* slurred six notes to a bow
Plus: Chromatic scale starting on Bb			separate bows *or* slurred two crotchet beats to a bow
Diminished 7th starting on G			

Major tonal centre

When the examiner requests a major tonal centre, the candidate should play in succession:

> The major scale
> The major arpeggio
> The dominant 7th starting on that note and resolving onto the tonic
> (to be prepared with separate bows and slurred two crotchet beats to a bow)

Minor tonal centre

When the examiner requests a minor tonal centre, the candidate should play in succession:

> The melodic minor scale
> The harmonic minor scale
> The minor arpeggio

Technical exercises (from memory) [♩ = 100]:

a) D major in thirds:

b) Eb major in sixths:

c) D major in octaves:

d) E major scale on one string:

or **iii) Orchestral extracts** (music may be used):

Candidates to prepare 1a *or* 1b; 2a *or* 2b; and 3a *or* 3b (three extracts in total).

The candidate will choose one extract to play first; the examiner will then select one of the remaining two prepared extracts to be performed.

The extracts are contained in *The Orchestral Violinist book 2* (ed. Rodney Friend) published by Boosey & Hawkes (9790060115967).

1a. Sibelius: Symphony no. 2 [IV Finale], page 7 (bar 1 to 1st note of bar 25) 1b. Wagner: Die Meistersinger von Nürnberg [Overture], page 24 (bars 97 to 100)	for tone and phrasing
2a. Beethoven: Egmont [Overture], page 39 (bar 309 to 1st note of bar 317) 2b. Copland: Appalachian Spring Suite, page 49 (fig. 24 to 1st note of fig. 25)	for bowing
3a. Beethoven: Egmont [Overture], page 39 (bar 287 to 1st note of bar 301) 3b. Stravinsky: Pulcinella Suite [8b. Finale], page 35 (two bars before fig. 105 to fig. 107)	for left hand technique

Supporting tests – candidates to prepare i) *and* ii)

i) sight reading	**ii) aural** *or* **improvisation**

Please refer to the current syllabus for details on all elements of the exam.